MW01168376

CHILDREN WHO COME AND GO

CHILDREN WHO COME AND GO

Vera James

UNIQUE EUPHONY

Publishing Group

Copyright © 2011 Vera James

ISBN Softcover 978-0-578-08162-5

Copyright © "SAM" is a copyrighted article of

The Ledger-Enquirer, January 16, 1983

All rights reserved. No part of this book may be reproduced or transmitted in any form or any means, electronic or mechanical, including photocopying, recording, or by any information storage and retrieval system, without permission in writing from the publisher.

This book was printed in the United States of America

To order additional copies of this book, contact:

Unique Euphony Publishing Group

706 - 577 - 3197

www.uniqueeuphony.com

inquiries@uniqueeuphony.com

Edited by Barbara Pierce

Layout & Cover Design by Tom Cody

In Dedication:

To the many people who have touched Samuel's life in some way, thank you so much for what you have done for him. Whether you took care of him in the hospital, lent him your ear, braided his hair, guided him through his many challenging tasks, taught him in school and Church, played with him, cried with him or prayed for him; from the bottom of our hearts, we appreciate all you have done for him.

Vera James

Acknowledgements

Giving honor and glory to God and His Son the Lord and Savior Jesus Christ without whom I wouldn't exist and our son's story would not be told.

Thanks go to my family, McCartha Drive Church of Christ members, supporters and friends of The Sickle Cell Foundation of Georgia, Inc., Association of Sickle Cell Lower Chattahoochee Region in Columbus, Georgia for all the love and support given to our family and to Samuel while he was with us.

Love and appreciation to my husband Reuben, who has been a true hus"band", holding things together at home which enabled me to nurture Samuel all of his 35 years.

Thanks to the staff, customers and friends of The Chattahoochee Valley Libraries, who listened, supported me at work and who made me feel "full" and complete.

This book is meant to be informative yes, but it is also therapeutic for me after saying "good-bye" to Samuel just three weeks ago.

Writing a story of Samuel's life as he lived it is encouraging to me and to those who are dealing with this debilitating disease or with an offspring, spouse or another relative who has sickle cell anemia. Samuel learned to live with his condition and cope with his episodes of crisis. He told me often that it was not easy but he was a real trooper and he held up under the weight of physical exhaustion and pain that plagued his body when his blood cells began to sickle.

PSALMS 23

The Lord is my shepherd, I shall not want. He maketh me to lie down in green pastures: he leadeth me beside the still waters. He restoreth my soul: he leadeth me in the paths of righteousness for his name's sake. Yea, though I walk through the valley of the shadow of death, I will fear no evil: for thou art with me; thy rod and thy staff they comfort me. Thou preparest a table before me in the presence of mine enemies: thou anointest my head with oil; my cup runneth over. Surely goodness and mercy shall follow me all the days of my life: and I will dwell in the house of the Lord forever.

II Cor. 5:1

For we know that if our earthly house of this tabernacle were dissolved, we have a building of God, an house not made with hands, eternal in the heavens.

A Tribute to My Brother

I'm okay. I just try and make it through my day. Seems the clouds don't wanna go away.

I'm okay. I tell myself this so that the tears won't stay. That's what they tell me to say.

I'm okay. Someday, someday, I really will be okay.

Tiffany James

July 24, 2010

-- "CHILDREN WHO COME AND GO" --

The Effects of Sickle Cell Disease

In Africa, The families affected by this crippling disease thought it to be a curse of the spirits. The children afflicted with the condition were thought to die to drive out evil spirits from the family to protect them from the evil curse.

They were called ogbanjes, which meant "children who come and go". They did chants and special dances to drive the evil spirits away.

Contents

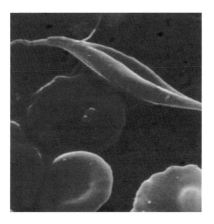

-- WHAT IS SICKLE CELL ANEMIA AND ITS SYMPTOMS? --

Sickle cell anemia (disease) is an inherited blood cell anomaly that links people geographically who are primarily of African, Mediterranean, or Southwest Asian ancestry, and its effects are widespread. The effects of the genetic disorder sickle cell anemia may be debilitating, restrictive and life threatening.

A defective gene that produces an abnormal form of hemoglobin causes blockages in red blood cells that pass through tiny blood vessels. Painful episodes occur when the blood cells form a sickle shape. Insufficient blood supply to organs impairs their function. Loss of blood flow causes infections and anemia. Lack of oxygen in red blood cells due to infections by microorganisms can also affect the onset of a painful crisis. According to Bloom who stated, "The most common complications involve the spleen, the eyes and the chest".

The bones and other areas of the abdomen are also affected

by bouts of painful crises. Blood cells that are destroyed during sickling need to be replaced in the bone marrow. Pain is caused by the inability of the sickled red blood cells to move through the sinusoids of bones. Circulation is impaired by this process. Hand foot syndrome, characterized by swelling in the hands and feet is common in young children with sickle cell disease. Other bones in the body may be affected by sickling as a person matures, and many times bone replacement surgery is necessary. Painful episodes of sickling in the bones can last for a few hours, a few days, or even for several weeks.

The abdomen is another area that is especially affected by the onslaught of excruciating pain in sickle cell disease. In the abdomen, the spleen may become enlarged and it may also shrink as a result of sickling of red blood cells. Also located in the abdomen, the spleen excretes excessive amounts of bilirubin during a crisis.

Insufficient oxygen in the red blood cells as they pass through the blood vessels in the chest cause severe pain and difficulty breathing. The chests of sickle cell patients are often narrower than normal and the heart is often larger. Lung disease such as pneumonia may be life threatening.

The lifestyle of a person who has sickle cell anemia is often restrictive. Excessive physical exertion may precipitate a painful crisis. Children may become lethargic in school while participating in activities during physical education.

Psychological stress is common in patients who cope with sickle cell disease. Emotional stress adversely affects sickle cell patients on a continual basis. Family relationships are often strained by the continual bouts of painful episodes experienced by the sickle cell patient. Moral support by family and friends and a support group may be beneficial in promoting good self esteem, which is so vitally important to sickle cell patients.

Sickle cell disease can be debilitation both physically and mentally; however, with sufficient medical care, proper nutrition and a good support system, a person can lead a relatively normal life.

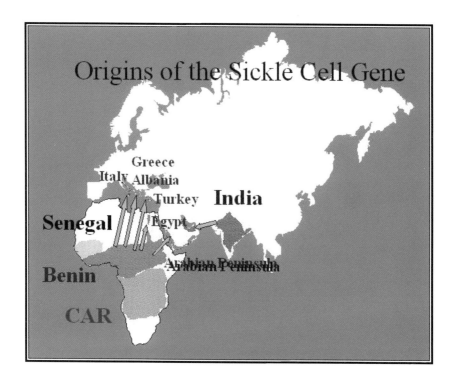

-- THE HISTORY OF SICKLE CELL ANEMIA --

In 1904, Walter Clement Noel left Grenada and moved to Chicago to attend Dental School. Later that year he was diagnosed with a type of anemia. In 1910, a publication was printed by Dr. James Herrick about Noel's specific type of anemia. It was later called sickle cell anemia.

Sickle cell anemia is an inherited disease that affects people from many racial ethnic backgrounds.

In the U.S. many people are carriers of the sickle cell trait who are not African American; dispelling the idea that sickle cell anemia is a black disease. Sickle cell disease and other hemoglobin variants have been found in descendants of Italians, Arabs, Caribbeans, Latin Americans, Greeks and other racial ethnic groups from the Mediterranean Sea area. Sickle cell anemia is an international health problem and a global challenge.

It is vitally important for everyone to be tested for sickle cell anemia because this disease has no limits as to its widespread effects.

In the U.S., Sickle Cell Disease occurs 1 in every 2,500 births, which is greater than that of any other condition detected by newborn screening. Data is available that supports the fact that sickle cell anemia can affect many races.

-- SICKLE CELL ANEMIA TIMELINE --

1846 - The first modern description of Sickle Cell Anemia is reported by R. Lebby, an American doctor.

1910 - Dr. James B. Herrick publishes the first medical report on sickle cell anemia. He discovered the sickle cell shape as he examined a sample of blood under the microscope.

1917 - Dr. Victor Emmel publishes a family history of sickle cell anemia.

1922 - Dr. Verre Mason becomes the first to use the term sickle cell anemia.

1923 - John Huck studies heredity's role in Sickle Cell Anemia based on two families.

1927 - Drs. E. Vernon and Elizabeth Gillespie show that low oxygen levels cause red blood cells to sickle.

1933 - Dr. Lemuel W. Diggs describes two forms of the disease: Sickle cell anemia and sickle cell trait.

1940 - Dr. Irving Sherman reports that sickling of red blood cells without oxygen is caused by a change in the molecules of hemoglobin.

1945 - Dr. Linus Pauling discovers that an abnormal form of hemoglobin was the cause of the sickling in sickle cell patients.

1948 - Janet Watson finds that blood of newborns does not sickle, namely fetal hemoglobin in red blood cells.

1956 - Dr. Vernon Ingram discovers that the difference between normal and abnormal hemoglobin lies in a single amino acid.

1978 - British scientist Richard Anthony Flavell maps the human genes that code for hemoglobin, demonstrating that sickle cell anemia is caused by a mutation in the DNA sequence of one gene.

1984 - The University of Chicago Medical Center reports its first bone marrow transplant for sickle cell treatment.

1986 - The National Heart and Lung Blood Institute reports that daily doses of penicillin are effective in preventing serious infections in children.

1987 - The National Institutes of Health recommends widespread newborn screening for sickle cell anemia.

1995 - Dr. Samuel Chararcle reports that the anticancer drug hydroxyurea reduces the pain of sickle cell anemia.

1998 - The first unrelated donor cord blood transplant is performed for sickle cell anemia.

1998 - The food and drug administration (FDA) approves hydroxyurea, the first drug used to prevent pain crises in adult patients with sickle cell anemia.

2000 - Research begins into new ways of treating sickle cell anemia, including the interaction of proteins in regulating globin production, somatic gene replacement therapy, and more optimal stem cell transplants.

2006 - A study sponsored by the FDA begins to determine if statins can help prevent injury to blood vessels.

2007 - A study sponsored by the National Heart, Lung and Blood Institute begins to collect, test and store blood and DNA samples from children and adults with sickle cell anemia to study the role that genes play in the disease. All states and the District of Columbia now routinely test newborns for sickle cell disease. Researchers report that induced pluripotent stem (ips) cells correct sickle cell anemia in mice.

-- SAMUEL SPEAKS --

My name is Samuel James. I am a twenty six year old black man with Sickle Cell Anemia.

My mother has asked me to write about my life and Sickle Cell.

For the most part, my life is happy. I don't have much wealth, but I have a 17 month old daughter who is always happy to see me and a 5 year old son who is named after me. It sometimes becomes difficult to care for them when I am in pain. My pain is chronic. I feel pain every day. I experience severe pain. This may be hard for some readers to understand. I am not completely uncomfortable; when I have pain medicine to take I am usually just fine. But then the time comes when I run out of medicine before my doctor thinks I should. I see my doctor once a month. She gives me what she thinks is a monthly supply of pain medicine. She gives me oxycontin 80 mg. I am to take one pill every 12 hours as needed for pain. This was fine when I first started taking the medicine, but just like any other human my body has built up a tolerance. Now a monthly supply will last two weeks, if I am lucky. I can't tell my doctor this. If I do, she will say I am abusing the drug and fire me. That means she will not treat me anymore. In her mind, if I need more than two of those pills a day to control my pain, I am a filthy drug addict who deserves no respect or consideration. This has happened to me many times over the years. Like an animal in the wild, I have learned to adapt. I must fabricate my real feelings to every person in the medical field that I come in contact with because this disease never, ever takes a break. No one understands. I don't expect them to. People offer all kinds of solutions. "You need Jesus," they say. "Take more vitamins". "Exercise more". "Meditate". "Eat more red meat". "Rub aloe all over", "Put garlic in your ears".

I am sure you readers catch my point.

Narcotic pain medicine, more specifically oxycontin 80 mg. is what works for my pain. People act so funny when they hear you take Narcos(narcotics) on a pretty regular basis like I do. You should see the look on medical professionals faces when I am in the Emergency Room and they have given me 400 mg. of Demerol and 150 mg. of Benadrl and I can stand and walk the same way that I could when I came in. They seem to not understand how my tolerance for pain medicine is so high. They are offended that I have been given so much narcotic pain medicine and I am not dead. What do they expect? My disease is a perfect example of how the human body adapts to survive. If you know the history of the disease, then you know what I mean.

Sometimes, I think of taking my own life; yes, suicide. It is really uncomfortable when I am in pain. I HATE IT. It makes me sick and angry and bitter when I am in pain and no one wants to do anything about it. What can I do? I am 26 and I want to do so many things for myself, my son and my daughter, my wife and my family. But when I am in pain with nothing to take for it, that is all I can do, is to be in pain. What does it all mean? When does it come to an end? Well, it depends on what a person will do to fulfill one's needs. Must I sway from the normal life I wish to lead in order for that life to be a comfortable one? I have done things that I'm not proud of. Those I will not mention for reasons that are probably quite obvious. Someday, hopefully there will be a cure for this dreadful, awful disease that I have. In the meantime, I must live with it and try to do the best that I can to maintain a normal life even though my condition makes it very difficult for me to sustain myself on a daily bases. My family is there for me but most of the time I just depend on myself. My children are the joy in my life and I want to be able to watch them grow up and become adults. Even if I don't make it, I want them to know that their daddy loves them very much.

Samuel James. 2001

In response to Samuel's story, I made some suggestions to help and support him as he strives for normalcy in his life.

Samuel, how can I help you?

1. Prepare delightful, delectable mouth watering meals to suit your appetite. (include anti-sickling foods)

2. Assist you with care of your children when possible.

3. Provide housing and assistance with day to day upkeep.

4. Aid Nelsa (Samuel's wife), with home management, such as budgeting, shopping, cleaning, cooking, wholesome educational, informative reading material. Videos.

5. Moral support including devotionals, relaxation activities such as family gatherings (at homes or parks). Saturdays/Sundays. Playing games such as checkers. Working puzzles, watching videos, volleyball, tennis, soccer, walking at parks or at the Riverwalk.

6. Writing the manuscript for the book on Sickle Cell Anemia

April 21, 2001

-- HIS EARLY YEARS --

When Reuben and I first learned that Samuel was anemic, he was a one year old bubbly baby. He didn't seem to be sickly in any way. Visits to his Pediatrician and several blood tests later, the results were that he was diagnosed as having Sickle Cell Anemia. As his parents, we were asked to be tested by having a specific blood test and the results confirmed that we were indeed carriers. Both my husband and I have a trait of Sickle Cell Anemia. Neither one of us knew much about Sickle Cell Anemia before nor had we been screened to confirm that we were carriers of the sickle cell gene.

We knew we had a tremendous hill to climb not only to become better informed about the disease but most importantly, how to take care of our son with this devastating condition. We moved our family to Columbus, Georgia so that we would be closer to Reuben's family and in search of treatment and advice on how to care for our special child. Thankfully, Samuel's siblings don't have the disease and they are not carriers of the sickle cell gene.

Our children made friends easily and one of our oldest son's friends who lived around the corner from us, told his parents about our family and our special child. His mother was a reporter for the Columbus Ledger and Enquirer and she wanted to do a story about Samuel and Sickle Cell Anemia.

Once a date and time was established, Mrs. Kaffie Sledge came to our home and she interviewed us. She took notes as we shared with her how Samuel was dealing with his condition and how we as a family loved and cared for him. Pictures were also taken for an article that was to be published in the Columbus Ledger Enquirer.

Mrs. Sledge wrote the following article about Samuel and Sickle Cell Anemia. It was printed in the Columbus Ledger Enquirer on January 16, 1983.

SAM

Though small for his age, Sam James looks and acts like any other normal 7-year old. But ticking away inside him is a blood disease that could kill him before doctors discover a cure. The disease is sickle cell anemia.

Vera James was four months pregnant when she developed abdominal pains so severe that she had to be hospitalized for a week. Doctors thought the pains were related to her pregnancy and wanted to perform an abortion, but she said no. A month later the problem reoccurred. This time it became life threatening. Doctors kept Mrs. James in the hospital two weeks, giving her only a 50-50 chance of survival. Baffled by her ailment, they again considered abortion but thought it was too risky at that point. As mysteriously as it arrived, though, the pain went away and Mrs. James had no further complications during her pregnancy.

The doctors never diagnosed her condition. But today Mrs. James is certain those two incidents were related to sickle cell anemia because the child she was carrying, Samuel has the disease.

Sam, who turns 8 Jan. 30, was diagnosed as anemic when he was 8 months old and by the time he was 1, his parents learned he had sickle cell anemia, an inherited blood disease.

After Mrs. James discovered Sam had sickle cell anemia, she says she went on an information-seeking rampage. "I read all the books I could find, and eight years ago there weren't many. I went to the public library. I went to medical libraries. I read every article, every pamphlet I could get my hands on. In one way I learned a lot about sickle cell — in another way I learned nothing."

What Mrs. James, a former operating room technician, did learn is that there's no cure for her son's disease. And it may eventually kill him. The red blood cells in Sam's body are sometimes misshapen — sickled — and therein lies the problem. A healthy blood cell looks like a donut. Its red color comes from millions of hemoglobin molecules. The hemoglobin picks up oxygen in the lungs and releases it to all parts of the body. Sometimes in Sam's body, however, the red blood cells become sickled — shaped like new moons — and cannot pass easily through blood vessels. These deformed cells clog small blood vessels, restricting oxygen flow to internal organs, causing parts of the organs to die from lack of oxygen, says Dr. Antonio Rodriquez, a Columbus hematologist. This causes pain and illness — crises — in the child. Repeated crises can be fatal.

"About one in every 400 to 600 black Americans has sickle cell anemia," says Andrew Skolnick, March of Dimes science writer. "And about one in 10 American blacks carries the sickle cell gene (also referred to as having the sickle cell trait)." Skolnick says it's a common misconception that the sickle cell gene is confined to black people. "This gene is also carried by some people of Arabian, Greek, Maltese, Sicilian, Sardinian and southern Asian ancestry. It is a gene that arose (over many generations) in these populations as protection against malaria," he says.

At birth a child with sickle cell, such as Sam, is protected by fetal hemoglobin. But by the end of his first year, this protection has ceased to function. Rodriguez says scientists are trying to find a way to keep the fetal hemoglobin working in sickle cell patients. But currently there is no cure for sickle cell, as doctors told Sam's parents.

"The doctors said there was nothing they could do," says Mrs. James. "They couldn't give us a life expectancy. We were simply told to be very careful with him – make sure he got good medical care – because he could die from the simplest of illnesses.

"When we learned Sam had sickle cell, we went through all the tears and emotions. We talked to our parents and other relatives, our friends. But other people get tired of hearing about your problems, and my husband, Reuben, and I learned pretty quickly that we were on our own. "At first friends listen and feel sorry, but then you get the feeling they think you are crazy – overreacting. It's like they are saying, "The kid has a cold, so what?" she says. But a person with sickle cell has low resistance to infections. And infections can trigger or worsen a crisis. A person with sickle cell can die as a result of a simple illness such as a cold, Mrs. James says. Sam has several crises a month — mostly minor ones, his mother says. "Maybe one or two big ones a year," she says. "Infections, fatigue, over exertion and unusual stress will bring on a crisis... So we try to keep as much of this out of Sam's life as possible." A sickle cell anemia crisis is characterized by severe pain in the chest, abdomen, arms and legs. These pains can last for a few hours or two to three weeks, Mrs. James says. Motivated by the saying, "You are what you eat," Mrs. James decided that Sam's best defense against crises was a healthy body that could fight back. "So I cook natural foods and limit use of processed foods and preservatives. Fresh fruits and juices are what I give the children for snacks," she says. Sam, save for his illness, acts like a normal 7-year old boy — all 3 feet 6 inches and 40 pounds of him. Sickle cell slows growth, too. He can be seen bouncing up and down the streets around his home at 909 Bunker Hill Road in Columbus. "But if Sam's eyes start getting yellow (jaundice) — the sign of a crisis — we start working on him immediately," his father says. "Since a crisis really means that his body isn't getting enough oxygen, we give him water because it contains oxygen. We also take him to a window and try to get him to breathe deeply. After that, it's just rest and water and other liquids." Says Mrs. James, "We use a lot of psychology, not pity. We encourage him to make himself well." The Jameses say parents of children with sickle cell are on guard 24 hours a day, seven days a week, watching for sores that aren't healing properly, swollen feet and hands and tending sore throats and painful joints — all symptoms of sickle cell. "It's like your life is on hold," Mrs. James says. "We go from one (sickle cell) crisis to another, praying that Sam will bounce back. We love Sam and we want to take care of him and protect him, but Sam is growing up and he has to learn to depend on himself. He has to learn to take care of himself because we may not always be around." Sam's fairly self-sufficient, his mother says. "If he starts to feel sick, or has trouble breathing, He'll drink some water and go rest for a while," she says. "Later he might tell me about it. Sometimes he'll come home from school and tell me that his stomach started to hurt (another sign of possible sickle cell crisis) but he didn't tell the teacher, because he didn't want to come home." Sam is a second grader at Dawson Elementary School. He missed a few weeks of school last year, but this year his mother says he's aiming for perfect attendance. "Sam is a good student and we encourage him, because when he grows up he'll have to depend on his brain – not his strength – for a living," Mrs. James says. Because both Reuben and Vera James have the sickle cell trait their chances of having three children with normal hemoglobin were statistically remote. But Sam's sister, Tiffany, 6, and his brothers Reuben, 11, and Eric, 9, have normal blood, Mrs. James says. "At least we beat the odds once," she says. "We're still trying to figure out how a girl from Pittsburgh and a guy from Fort Mitchell (Ala.) met in San Jose and had a child with sickle cell." Blood tests are available for sickle cell screening at local health departments. The health departments also provide genetic counseling for potential parents who have the sickle cell trait. The Jameses didn't know about sickle cell anemia, they say, until they were told Sam had it. Today they say they might have risked having children even if they'd known the risk they were taking. Statistics indicate that one-half of all sickle cell patients die before they reach 40, but hematologist Rodriguez doesn't agree. "There's a 56 —year-old woman in Savannah who has 12 children and has never been in the hospital a day in her life," he says. "There's no record of all the sickle cell patients who do not fit the statistics."

The Jameses say they live each day for itself. "We really have no time to think about numbers and ages. We just want Sam and all our children to have the best possible life — for as long as it lasts," Mrs. James says.

Kaffie Sledge

Ledger Enquirer

January 16, 1983

-- GROWING UP WITH THE FAMILY --

Samuel enjoyed school and he did his best to make good grades. He tried to please his teachers and he made friends easily. He did however have issues with his classmates telling him that he was going to die. This presented a challenge for him and the whole family. His siblings very often defended him in school when the other students laughed and jeered at him because of his small stature. When Sam was in Kindergarten, his teacher's name was Ms. Green. I remember him telling me that he wanted to marry Ms. Green. I smiled at his comment and as is evident from the class picture that was taken that year of his class at Dawson Elementary, he seemed rather content to be in her class-room. He had a very good year in her kindergarten class and that set the precedence for him to experience high self esteem throughout all of his elementary and middle school years. A positive attitude and high self esteem are so important for sickle cell patients because their emotional well being plays a great part in the recovery from periods of crises.

Sam was introduced to a very kind gentleman who befriended him when he was nine years old. His name was Jak Rothschild. Through this friendship, he learned that although there are peo-ple in the world who act adversely toward others, there also exist compassionate human beings. His dad and I were pleased that Sam was happy and that he had a mentor to encourage him at that time. Another important person in Sam's young life was our former minister of the congregation that we attend. Bro. Willie Bradford, Jr. had a tremendous influence on Samuel's spiritual life. He encouraged his growth in his study of the Bible. Bro. Roger Brawner noticed Samuel's gift as a young preacher and he suggested that someone get him a stool to stand on in order for others to see his face as he delivered his talk. His dad promptly made him a step stool and whenever we traveled to other congregations and Samuel was chosen to speak, we were prepared. He was able to share the lesson that he had studied and this pleased him greatly. To other members of the Church of Christ, I was known as "the mother of Samuel James, the young man who preaches."

I sincerely believe that Sam experienced fewer episodes of crises during this period of his life because of his devotion to the Word of God and sharing with others his faith in God. He not only spoke in Church but he shared at school as well. I remember discussing evolution and creation with Samuel and trying to help him in his studies as he dealt with the teaching of evolution in the Public School System. We had numerous conversations on how to handle spirituality in a secular world. Samuel became very knowledgeable in not only handling the Word of God from a child's perspective but also in how he dealt with his special condition. My husband and I let him know that he was special and that his talents must be used to help him cope with his physical condition throughout his life. We also encouraged him to walk by the faith that he had in the Lord and in his dear son, Jesus Christ. Our family experienced great joy as we shared a harmonious life at home and when conflicts and issues arose, we peaceably dealt with the situations. Samuel's siblings were bothered at times by all the attention that was lavished on him, but we included them in whatever we did as a family. Whether we went on outings in Columbus or took trips out of town, all of our children were included. We taught Samuel to share with others and that he shouldn't gloat because of the attention that was being focused on him from time to time. It was just as important for his siblings to have a high self esteem as it was for Samuel's mental state and this we reminded him of when it was necessary.

 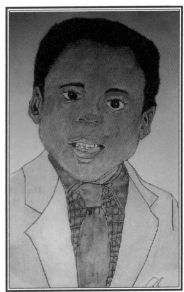

Portrait of Samuel by his
brother Reuben

<u>Special Memories of Sam</u>

I remember as a kid my brother Sam and I would ride these little 50 CC scooters that he had bought us, all over Columbus. People would always laugh and smile at the sight of us coming on our scooters, while wearing real motorcycle helmuts! It was a crazy sight. I loved those moments riding alongside my older brother, whom I had become accustomed to calling my "lil" brother because I was always just a bit bigger than him. But anyone who knew us knew he was really my big brother. As a teenager, Sam and I were inseparable, and you never saw me without him. And vice versa. I watched in awe as my "lil" brother would captivate an entire room with his very presence. We were hometown celebrities because of his incredible talent to sing, or dance, or just tell a story. I would later watch from the wings as he made a whole crowd stand still as he sang his heart out in a local talent show, and in that moment I was so proud to be this guy's little sister. Sam and I began to grow up and grow apart a little, but I never forgot all those days he would go riding with me on that scooter I cherished so much. One day as our older brother Reuben was driving me to work, I spotted a real motorcycle out front of a pawn shop. My eyes lit up and I begged him to stop the car. He relented and pulled up to the shop. I got out of the car, running straight over to the bike. It looked so big and dangerous. Reuben asked me, " So, are you gonna buy it or what?" I responded, "I wouldn't know how to even start it up!" Being my big brother he retorts," So what, you can learn!" With my newfound confidence I walk inside and put on as much maturity as I could muster into my 19 yr old voice. "Excuse me sir; how much for the bike out front?" The pawnbroker walked over to my side of the counter and while eyeing me doubtfully responds "I'm selling it for someone else and it's nineteen hundred." I gasped. I had no idea these things were so expensive. I then thought about going outside and telling my big brother I had punked out and decided to buy it. "Can I put it on layaway?" I said to the man in a small voice that wasn't so mature anymore. "Sure!" he said quickly. "Just give me two hundred dollars down and you can pay every week until you pay it off." I reached inside my pocket slowly praying I had enough. I peeled off the twenties slowly and handed them over. After counting the bills to make sure it was all there, the man handed me paperwork to fill out and a receipt. I walked out of the pawnshop thinking, "What have I done?"

Ninety days later I returned to the pawnshop to make the final payment of many I had been making to pay off this bike I wanted  so badly. The pawnshop owner asked if I knew how to ride and I shook my head no. He then offered to have his wife follow us and he would drive the bike to my house himself and drop it off. Once we reached my mother's yard, he parked the motorcycle, got off of it, and handed me the key. I looked at it and just blinked like a little kid. Oh how small I felt in that moment. Shyly I asked him, "Can you show me how to start it?" He looked at me as if I was an alien and began to show me. After he gave me the basics of how to start it and shift from one gear to the next, he jumped in the truck with his wife and was gone. I stood there in my mother's driveway just looking at MY bike. It was mine! But I had to learn to drive it. What good was having a bike if you couldn't ride? Sam! Sam ain't scared of nothing, I thought to myself! I raced to the front door and ran to Sam's room. "Hey, I just got my bike from the pawnshop and they just dropped it off!" He stood up immediately and said, "Where is it?" I told him it was outside and to come with me and I would show him. He followed me outside and walked over to the bike. I looked up at him for his approval that I needed so badly. He nodded and said it looked cool. I felt relieved just a bit, but one more thing lay in wait to be asked. "Can you help me learn how to ride?" He said very easily, "Sure." So we set about together learning how to ride a motorcycle we knew nothing about. I had never seen my brother so happy as when he successfully taught me how to ride and he learned to ride too in the process. I will never forget the look on his face as he learned to start it and finally started to shift the gears in the right way. As soon as he learned something new about the bike, he made sure he showed me too. I will always love my brother for teaching me what would become one of my favorite hobbies over the years. He didn't ride as much as I did as we got older and I bought bike after bike, but we always shared that same love of motorcycles. I have never been closer to anyone in my life as I was to my "lil" bro Sam. And I doubt I ever will be. I will cherish every memory I have of him, and the ones I hold dear to my heart are my bike lessons with Sam. He was the best teacher I ever had.

Love you always,

your lil sis, Tiff

Tiffany James   August 2010

-- *LIVING WITH SICKLE CELL ANEMIA* --

The members of a family with a child who has sickle cell anemia must often times delay their wishes and desires in order to meet the needs of the sickle cell defier. I use the term defier to point out that when we first learned about Samuel's condition, we taught him to maintain a proactive attitude throughout his life. We worked with him as he dealt with each crisis and let him know that he was loved beyond measure. Above all, we stressed that God would guide him throughout his life every step of the way and that he could live a fulfilling and healthy life as long as it lasted. However, Samuel was self willed and determined to do things his way. He would often hide his fears and anxieties many times which precipitated the onset of crises. With patience and support his dad and I were readily available to guide him through each physical challenge. We used firmness and persuasive coaxing to encourage him to make himself well and to not get discouraged because he had to take a back step when it came to participating in physical activities with his siblings or with his classmates in school. Samuel was encouraged to eat healthy snacks and to drink plenty of water. He welcomed rest periods because he learned early that when he became tired, he needed to lie down. As a family, we engaged in activities that Samuel could do without stress or strain. The children played games; we went on outings such as visits to the museum, the library or to a symphony concert. Our family vacationed whenever it was possible and we were reenergized and refreshed when we returned home. Samuel was eager and ready to go anywhere we went and he seemed quite happy to engage in as many activities as he was able to. My husband and I always made adjustments to our plans whenever he had a crises or he needed to rest.

Sundays were always exciting because Samuel looked forward to going to Bible Study and Worship Service with the family. His face seemed to light up as he asked questions and interacted with the other students in the class. He enjoyed the singing and he was eager to lead songs when he was asked to participate in the young brothers' service. Later he began to give talks during the young brothers' services and this activity was very stimulating to him.

As parents, Reuben and I were constantly challenged to not only deal with each day's obstacles in handling Samuel's condition, but we had to prayerfully look to the future and what lie ahead for Samuel. We encountered obstacles from time to time as we sought help for our special child. The following details some of the challenges we experienced:

"The phone rang; it was an agent from an insurance company. He called to give us the sad news once again that our son would not qualify for coverage under their plan because all Sickle Cell Anemia patients are excluded. Tears streamed down my cheeks once again as we sought help to obtain insurance for our son and our family. We were on limited finances at that time and we were overwhelmed with doctor's fees. It was truly a blessing that I was able to use the medical knowledge and experience I received when I worked as an O.R. Technician in dealing with our son's condition. Although doors were closed, we continued with our quest to help our children live healthy lives and help to create an environment for Samuel that was nurturing and fulfilling."

Support from extended family members was always encouraging. I remember the following conversation as though it were today.
May 10, 1983, I talked to my sister in California yesterday. Appar-
ently she had been screened for sickle cell and the blood test re-
vealed that she too had a trait of sickle cell anemia. "Not to worry, I
told her. The information that I have been fortunate enough to have
gathered can help you." We compared notes over the phone and to
our surprise; we realized a similarity in our overall intolerance to
certain foods. My sister advised me to research certain food allergies
that Samuel might be susceptible to and to look at some anti-sickling
foods as well. Herbs that might be beneficial are yellow dock root for
cleansing the blood, sassafras for relaxation, catnip for many conditions such as stomach problems, rose hips for allergies, eucalypus for
colds, red sage for cleansing the blood, red sage- a cure all and for
liver cleansing and golden seal- a cure all. We also talked about preparing nutritious foods to help strengthen Sam's body. The conversation was very comforting to me and I began to research foods that
would be helpful for dealing with sickle cell and other maintenance
measures for sickle cell patients.

Many times the sickle cell defier's body is weaker than the aver-
age person's body making him/her more susceptible to common illnesses. When a child is in the formative years and he is shedding his baby
teeth, the primary teeth may come in behind the normal gum line.

During pollen season, children with sickle cell may have frequent colds and congestion. The child may develop pneumonia or a crises if colds are not taken seriously. Some treatment methods during these periods may be rubbing the chest at night with vicks vapo rub or methilatum. Tylenol may be given for a fever and a cough expectorant may be given when needed. Light exercise, fresh air and plenty of fluids such as water and juice might be given to the ill person to help him overcome his cold or congestion. He might also dress lightly and avoid drafts and extreme heat. Plenty of love and affection might be of benefit to the emotional well being of the sickle cell defier. As a child, Samuel was very receptive to correction and he was eager to obey. He was comforted by the presence of a family member at all times.

Mild to Moderate Bouts of Sickle Cell Crises

Samuel began to experience bouts of sickle cell crisis at the age of 6 years old. In 1982, I began to jot down when he experienced pain and what was necessary to do to give him some relief.

7/3/82 - Samuel experienced a mild crisis and he laid down for 30 min. He drank some water and juice and he seemed to feel better.

7/4/82 - Sam had stomach pain and I gave him some yellow root tea and cat nip tea. He rested for 30 min. and his pain subsided.

7/21-24/82 - Samuel was visiting his grandmother the first day of the crisis. When he came home I immediately began to give him liquids such as water, grape juice and grapefruit juice. I noticed that there was redness around the pupil of his eye that remained for several days. He managed to eat a soft cooked egg two days after the onset of pain. He soaked in the tub with tepid water and he dressed lightly. He was encouraged to play and ride his bike but not to the point of exhaustion. He spent most of the time for the first three days in bed but on Friday he was awake most of the day. I put Vaseline on his chapped lips and he ate some raisins for a snack, although earlier he regurgitated the oatmeal that I gave him.

2/4/83 - Samuel came in the house and complained that his stomach was hurting. I took notice of his condition because he rarely spoke of his pain unless it became unbearable. I put a heating pad on his stomach and he said that the heating pad increased the pain. He drank some water and then he rested for a while until he felt better.

2/18/83 - Samuel experienced pain in his legs and his stomach on and off most of the day. He told me about his pain episode after he came home from school.

3/15/83 - Samuel had chest, stomach and leg pain all day at school. He stayed in school all day but he told me about it when he got home. He was a very emotional child who needed to share how he felt about his pain.

4/10/83 - Sam told me that his gums hurt and I looked in his mouth. There was a white bump on his lower gum. I told him to gargle with salt water and then rinse his mouth with some mouth wash. In a few days the bump was gone but it reappeared later. I gave him lots of water and juice to flush the impurities out of his system.

Growing up, Samuel was a strong young man and he was conscientious about thinking things through. His wisdom far exceeded his years. He never let his condition hinder him, in fact he tried so much harder and he often succeeded because of his determination. There were discipline problems at times but his dad and I were firm with him on those occasions. We carefully taught him self control without using corporal punishment. We learned to be patient and gentle with all of our children. We spent many hours listening to them and talking to them. Family meetings and devotionals were scheduled and everyone in the family was in attendance. Having a close knit family was very helpful in dealing with Samuel's condition and he flourished as a result of the positive influence in the home. His dad and I worked with the counselors, teachers and principals in the schools that Samuel attended and we informed them about his unique condition. They were very understanding and supportive during his years in school. Samuel took care of his little sister and at times he advised her incorrectly. It was necessary to reprimand him about taking liberties with circumventing our parental instructions concerning his sister. He wasn't happy with this information, but he accepted it without further controversy or disciplinary measures. He responded with a written affirmation that he would not interfere with his dad's or my discipline of his sister. He also stated that he would not sass us or say, "Don't get mad"! He agreed to try to get along with all family members and that we would all show love, help and support each other. *8/28/89*

-- *SPREADING HIS WINGS* --

As Samuel matured and looked forward to the future, he sometimes made unwise decisions as most of us have in our lifetime. He
expressed a desire to do whatever he chose to do. He was free spirited
and sometimes he paid the penalty for not having the foresight of taking into account his condition. He was reared to have confidence in
himself and to strive to do the best that he could and to not be afraid
to tackle challenging tasks. Samuel used his wit, mental astuteness
and pleasing personality to win the hearts of many. This was one of
his greatest assets because as he matured, he began to embrace life ful-
ly and he accomplished some tremendous feats. One in particular was
his willingness to serve as a Counselor for the Sickle Cell Retreat in
Atlanta. He managed to take care of himself and counsel other youth
with Sickle Cell at the same time. He was cheerful and upbeat. He
entertained the attendees and one year before he became a counselor,
he won first place in a Talent Contest at the Sickle Cell Retreat. It was
my privilege to accompany him one year and volunteer as a Counselor
at the Retreat as well. His little brothers enjoyed listening to him as
he spoke, hanging on his every word. They really looked up to him
because he was "this tall handsome dud who was cool even though
he had Sickle Cell Anemia". Samuel was a good role model and the
other counselors knew that they could depend on him to keep the
youth straight... so to speak. It was refreshing to witness his positive
display of talent as he silently dealt with his pain.

Our Samuel soon became a man and he began to spread his wings…. Something to be expected as one grows up. He was a good student in school and although he stopped going to high school in the traditional sense, he did obtain his GED. He was nearing his 17th birthday and his emotions were often frazzled by the shenanigans of other youth his age. He was very mature and sometimes he just didn't feel well and he didn't want to share his discomfort with anyone. He'd much rather just be to himself until he felt better. He missed out on some of the social activities that his siblings attended and this often frustrated him. He compensated for his frequent alone time by reading and writing. He began writing in elementary school and he continued writing throughout his high school days. Here are a few of his writings that he wrote when he was in school:

The One Bad Thing about Birthdays

by Sam

I like birthdays. Mom always puts lots of frosting on my birthday cake. Everybody sings happy birthday. Then I blow out the candles and make a wish. That's the one bad thing about birthdays. I get to make only one wish. I wish I could make more wishes on my birthday. I wish my dad would say, Sam your bike is too little, you need a 3 speed. I wish my mom would say sure you can watch this movie called "V". I wish my big brother would say, "Come on along with us, Sam." All my friends think you're great. I wish my dentist would say, "You'll have to chew more bubble gum Sam, it's good for you." And the mail man will say, "All the mail is for you today, Sam". Birthdays are great, but I wish I didn't have to wait a whole year to make another birthday wish.

How I Would Feel If I Had Someone
Who Had Sickle Cell To Play With

by Sam

I would feel happy if someone with Sickle Cell played with me. I would bet we would get along most happily. I have met someone with Sickle Cell before. His name was Roger. We went to the same school together until the day when I got a letter that said for me to go to Georgetown Elementary School and he had to go to Eastway Elementary School. He was very nice to me, and I was very nice to him. We did not like the last day of school because we thought that would be the last time we saw each other and we were right. I have not seen him since. So now I do not have a person with Sickle Cell to play with. When Roger and I were together, we had the good times and the bad times, but when we were together, we were the happiest kids in the school. When I came in the classroom and sat down, he was the one to lift me up. He never, ever let me down. He was always happy and bright when he came in the classroom. We made good grades but we talked to each other a lot and sometimes we got in trouble for it.

What's The Matter Sam, Can't You Ride?

by Sam

When I was little I tried to ride a bike. Then I got Eric's bike out. I tried and I tried but I could not ride. I just kept falling down. When I got up, Steven passed by. My mother was babysitting him and Chris. And I asked him to help me. And he did, and when I learned, I rode fast. But I did not know how to turn. Then I learned to turn. Then a few months later I got my bike. Then a few months after that my sister got her bike. And me and daddy taught her how to ride. And it did not take too long. Then we rode together. The End

A few years later Samuel was selling newspapers on the corner of St. Mary's Rd. and the Bypass and he raised enough money to buy his very own bicycle. Sam was so very proud of his bike and he really took care of his bike. Samuel was happy and he didn't have many bouts with sickle cell crises so he was able to participate in several activities in school and also after school. He was in the 4-H club, the chorus, and he attended the boys club with his brothers. He tried to keep up with his brothers and he did a good job of keeping pace when he was well. He also took piano lessons along with his little sister.

-- *STRUGGLES AND PAINFUL EPISODES* --

In the previous chapters, I spoke of Samuel's bouts with Sickle Cell Anemia and how he dealt with his crises. During those years, his dad and I were able to help him deal with his crises and give him some relief. He was more receptive to the things that we told him to do in order to avoid having a crises and to basically take good care of himself. He ate the food that I cooked and while he lived at home, the atmosphere was for the most part, peaceful and quiet. He was able to relax and rest when he needed to and participate in activities that we as a family engaged in. However, as he grew up and became an adult, he began to engage in some of the activities that other youth engage in and sometimes he over extended himself. As I stated earlier, he wanted to do just what he wanted to do and there was no convincing him otherwise. We shared that it would be wise for him to modify his activities and diet in order to avoid stressful situations, over exertion, and to eat healthy foods.

January 21, 1995, I noted the events that took place while Samuel was in the hospital.

He had been in a coma for several days and we were praying that he would wake up. These notes explain the episode:

Sam is home now and my thoughts are slowly beginning to come together and I tried to make heads or tails of the whole ordeal.

What happened? That was my first reaction when I received a phone call from my daughter-in-law, Darlene. "Just get to the hospital quick and pick us up too on your way." How could I drive being so teary eyed. My mind was racing, my throat was dry and adrenalin was pumping so hard that I could hardly concentrate and drive. It was necessary to do what I had to do and face the matter at hand. We arrived at the hospital in a short time and we immediately went to the eighth floor MICU of the Medical Center. We were hoping to see our son right away and we walked toward the double swinging doors leading to the CCU unit. Before we were able to enter the room, the Chaplin, Mr. Lee a very kind sympathetic gentleman, asked us to walk around the short corner to the Pastoral Room. Samuel's doctor also accompanied us to the room. When we were all seated, Samuel's doctor explained that our son was very sick and that his condition had become life threatening. The hospital staff were doing all that they could do to make him comfortable. He was given several tests, antibiotics were administered in an effort to lower his extremely high temperature. We were asked if we had any questions. Sam's dad was concerned about his on-going care once he recovered. We were optimistic that the Lord would allow Sam to be revived and be whole again. We were escorted into the CCU unit to see Sam after the doctor had answered all of our questions. Half speechless, I touched my child and began to pray to God to spare his life. I was not ready to deal with his possible death. I had faith that God would grant all of us more time together. I thought back over the years and did a personal assessment of my role as a loving, supportive Mother. I continued to do the best that I could for all of our children. I knew that it would be God's decision as to

Samuel's outcome.

The first night was very difficult in that I walked and prayed all through the night. I talked softly to Samuel, not knowing whether he heard me or not. When the sun came up, I was so exhausted that I had to go home and rest for awhile. Once I freshened up and rested, I returned to Sam's bedside to pray and to softly encourage him to wake up. When I arrived at the hospital and approached his room, one of his specialists was examining him. He talked to me about his progress and he stated that he was slowly being allowed to breathe on his own with the respirator still assisting his breathing. The results from the tests that were taken came back negative but his temperature was still elevated. The following two days were spent in vigilance and prayer. Emotionally and physically, I gave our youngest son all the strength that I could muster. In a situation like critical illness, one doesn't think about not worrying, for it's hard to keep from falling apart when you see a loved one in such a debilitated helpless condition. By Friday, Sam was beginning to stir and my heart leaped for joy. Meningitis was ruled out and the first CAT scan was negative, all good signs. With the antibiotics still being administered, his temperature began to lower. I knew the Lord wasn't ready for him right then and he was given more time on this earth. I began to think of the conversations we would have once he was breathing on his own and the tubes were removed. He began breathing on his own and by Saturday, all the tubes were removed. After an adjustment period, Sam began to talk and he was back to his normal self. I returned to work on Tuesday, the day after Martin Luther King holiday. It was hard to focus on my job but with supportive co-workers present to offer kind words and listening ears, I completed that first day. After leaving work, I went to see Sam at the hospital. By Wednesday, he was settled in a room on the 6th floor and he was beginning to eat soft food.

He told me that he was very hungry because he hadn't eaten for a week. The next day, Thursday I brought Sam a lunch that consisted of fried chicken and all the trimmings. He could only eat the chicken. I was very happy to see him eat period! He continued to improve although I knew that it would be some time before he regained his strength. He came home on Friday, January 20, 1995. I wanted to give him a party but he declined because he just needed to rest. I understood and was just happy to have him home again. We love you Sam.

We agreed to share the work at home and to be more considerate of each other.

We would share expenses and communicate by leaving notes and choosing a time to talk.

We agreed to assist Samuel in his efforts to avoid having a crises by:

Playing music moderately and lowering our voices.

No altercations either verbally or physically.

Use moderation in all things in order to promote a peaceful co-existence.

Eating several small meals daily and balancing his diet with plenty of fresh fruits and vegetables.

Drink plenty of fluids such as juice and water.

He must get plenty of rest.

Help and support all family members.

Rest when pain begins in order to avoid more severe pain and hospitalization.

Take pain medication at home when necessary (Tylenol 3).

Some ideas for maintenance and improved health:

1. Get a journal and record each crises and what is going on at the time:

   a. Mental state of mind

   b. Activity at the onset of pain

   c. Location of pain

   d. Food or drink

   e. Persons present and circumstance

2. Talk to Dr. Walker about family counseling (support group meets the 4th Tues. of each month.

   a. Reasons for family counseling:

      Reasons for emotional outburst

3. Buddy system (find a partner that he can interact with).

4. Family meetings periodically (every two weeks).

-- COMING TO TERMS --

As a mother of a bright young man who is hindered in so many ways by a gripping, crippling, mind wrenching condition, let me share with you for a moment. My youngest son in my opinion, has a bright future. I have thought and I still believe he has promise. However, somehow, someway he must find a workable plan to manage his disease in order to experience some success in life. By now you are thinking, what is she talking about? This monster I am referring to is Sickle Cell Disease. It is a debilitation condition that permeates every fiber of a person's body who is afflicted with it. Research data has proven to be ineffective in dealing with this condition because without a cure or even relief from pain, a person constantly fears the onslaught of painful episodes. Information that my husband and I shared with a newspaper reporter some time ago, dealt with our experiences at that time. Since then our son has grown up and now that he has left the nest, and has started a family, he and his wife must cope with ongoing bouts of sickle cell crises.

When Samuel was in Elementary School, his care was handled at home. I retired from my position as a Surgical Technician so that I could take care of him. Many times I received phone calls from school stating that he was experiencing pain. I went to the school to pick him up. On the way home, I asked him to tell me how he felt. This helped to relieve some of the stress that he was experiencing whether from the pain of sickling of from some emotional challenge.

We shared and he seemed to relax. If he still felt pain when we got home, he drank some water and sometimes he relaxed in a tub filled with slightly warm water. This soothing bath helped quite a bit. Sometimes I would rub the area that caused him the greatest amount of pain and I would rock him in the rocking chair. I'd sing softly to him until he fell asleep. He often slept for several hours and when he woke up, his pain had subsided. When his pain did not go away after several hours of sleep, I would give him children's Tylenol.

As parents of a sickle cell patient, my husband and I provided a stable home, love and support which is so important for a person living with sickle cell. Emotional stress is heightened when needs are not being met and the onset of pain begins again as a result of the psychological anxiety experienced. In caring for a person who must live with this inherited disease which afflicts those of African, Mediterranean and Asian Indian ancestry as well as other nationalities, care givers must be supportive and sensitive to their needs. It is important to help build their self esteem and motivate them continually. A strong mind is the best defense against a condition that can affect so much of a person's body.

Samuel tried his best as a husband and a father, but he experienced many challenges and they were extremely difficult. He made every effort to support his family, to love and care for them. He was present and attentive when his children were infants and as they grew he was an engaged dad. It saddened Samuel that circumstances were of such that he wasn't as present with his first born as he was with his daughter and his youngest son. It grieved him so much that his condition prevented him from being present when his oldest son had

a game or a school function. He did attend his school occasionally
and had lunch with him. It was wonderful to see the two of them
together. Lil Sam not only was named after his dad but he looked so
much like him. When Lil Sam visited his dad and spent the night,
there was nothing better in life for his dad. He was with his son
and he was so very proud of him. Samuel doted on Lil Sam and he
bragged about his accomplishments as any proud father would do.
Although father and son didn't spend as much time as they might
have wanted to, it was the quality of the time that they spent together
that mattered the most. Lil Sam brought joy into his dad's life and
Lil Sam can be rest assured that his dad left an impressionable legacy
as a fighter and an achiever, a lover of all that is good and kind. No
matter what issues he had to deal with Samuel James held his head
high and accepted them like the astute man that he was. I'd like to
share one of his letters during his incarceration, which was due to a
misunderstanding, to say the least.

Dear Mother,

    Could you please send me pictures of everyone? Send pictures
of my kids, you, your hubby and my siblings. Just send four of them
at a time. I would be very much pleased if you could. It gets very
lonely in this jail. And I think I will probably be locked up for at least
a year. Please send the pictures and maybe some kind words.

Your son,

Samuel

April 19, 2005

My dear Samuel,

I came home from work today and checked the mailbox. I was pleased to have another letter from you. It was my intention to write you right back after you sent the first letter. This was after court on last Monday, but it didn't materialize. Anyway, better late than never. (smile) In response to your first letter, you seemed upbeat and encouraged and God knows I pray that you keep yourself like that as much as possible. It won't be long; those shackles of the jail will be coming off. Hold on! Those pictures of Samantha and Isaac are great. That guy is really talented. Especially Isaac, it looked just like him. Manthy looked a little older than she is on the picture. Like I said, if you're still there, tell him to draw a picture of you. Sit for the picture instead of him drawing you from the picture. Sam, we all love you too and we are doing all that we can to help alleviate the situation. I talked to Mr. Casto yesterday. He said that he did talk to the District Attorney, Michael Craig. Out of their discussion, he stated that Craig is sympathetic to your situation, because he had a similar situation. First of all, Casto said Craig would try calling Nelsa again and if he doesn't get a response from her, the case may be thrown out. Again when, I don't know. However, Casto said that he was going to try to get you out on bond, like he said before. He said that maybe it would be sometime this week. Sam, all we can do at this point is to wait on the Lord to intercede, touch somebody's heart and work in your behalf. Not just talk but also do something to cause your release and bring this situation to the table so it can be resolved. Life has a way of molding and shaping us. If we listen to the message of the trial we will understand what we need to do. I know it's hard for you to think at the present time, or plan for the future, but if you'll hold on and let God, he'll work it out in His time. You know, we pray to God and ask Him to help us, but sometimes we're not willing to wait on Him. I'm not just speaking about time either; I'm talking about once he answers our prayer, being content, like Paul with the outcome of our request. It's called faith and we need a lot of it in this life. Just waking up each day and doing the same ole things takes faith. Some-times, I get bored with that and bored with the same faces and bored with the same foods, clothes and routines, but I have to go in faith because that is God's will for my life. He lets me know when I study His Word how He orders my steps and why. Faith and trust in Him keeps me on the straight and narrow. I love Him and I want to obey Him. In that I am happy and content in spite of my difficulties from time to time. Like I said before, hold on, that's all we can do. Hold on to God's unchanging hand and He'll provide all that we need when we need it. I hope trust and pray that you share these few words with your fellow inmates because they too can be strengthened. About being watched so repeatedly, I'm sorry that you have no privacy. Dad and I are preparing for you to have privacy as we speak. Your room is almost ready. You can have your space and privacy so you can just chill out and relax. Sounds great huh? Well you deserve it. Hopefully we'll have that feast that you requested as well. I know you'll enjoy the Sorento also. You're a changed man and I believe you. With a new perspective in mind, I trust that you will be level headed and honor your commitment. I have been praying that the Lord would touch you in a mighty special way again and cause you to realize how He can use you with your gifts that He has blessed you with. With a comfortable environment and comfortable transportation, you can work wonders for the Lord in appreciation of how much He has blessed you. I'm still trying to make it to work.

Take care, and hang in there champ!

Love,

Mom

P.S. Dad said hi and hang in there.

-- HOPE FOR THE FUTURE --

Samuel's life after his incarceration became tumultuous continuously and it became more difficult for him to maintain his existence as a spouse. He and his wife separated but he was still very active in his children's lives. He took care of them whenever they came over to visit. They will always remember the special moments that they shared. Samuel grew tired but he never gave up. He enrolled at Columbus Technical Institute several times and took several courses. He didn't finish because of many absences. Samuel worked in customer service and his tenure with Pizza Hut was the longest that he held a position. Even though he was out because of illness many times, Patsy, his boss was very understanding. She allowed him to return to work even though he was often out for several weeks at a time. He was an engaged employee and he shared with us how he served his customers. We were very proud of Samuel's devoted and sincere spirit in his employment. His attitude sustained him during times of restriction due to his condition. Six months before he passed, Samuel filled out paperwork to attend Columbus State University and he was actively working with the Rehabilitation Center at the GDL here in Columbus.

During the winter of this year, Samuel's health began to decline and he was growing weaker but he persevered in spite of his frailties.

I was privileged to talk to a young lady who is living with Sickle Cell Anemia and her story mirrors Samuel's life.

We met at Mildred L. Terry Public Library on September 3, 2010. Before she arrived, I wrote a letter to her introducing myself and giving her feedback as to how important our meeting would be. The letter:

Hi Katrina,

My name is Vera James. Thank you for meeting with me today to share your experiences dealing with Sickle Cell Anemia. My son, Samuel James passed away in May of this year from complications related to Sickle Cell Anemia. He was also chemically dependent on several pain medications. This contributed to his steady decline in health since the first of this year. Samuel lived for 35 years and as he stated in his comments, most of his life he had joy. He obtained his GED, attended Columbus Technical College, and worked on several jobs until his health prevented him from working. He was married, later divorced and he was the father of 3 beautiful children. During the early years of Samuel's life, I was the main person who helped him deal with his condition. When he became sick and experienced crises, I gave him children's Tylenol and he'd lie down for awhile. He drank juice and other liquids and ate light food until his pain episodes diminished. Even though he wasn't able to do all that his siblings did physically, he still tried to do as much as he could.

Vera James

Ms. Murdix in sharing her story about living with Sickle Cell Anemia, reminded me so much of how Samuel lived with his condition.

Here is her story:

Katrina Murdix's episodes of crises became more frequent after she became an adult and moved out on her own. Her first job was at AFLAC where she worked for a period and then she accepted a position at CB&T. While she was working there, she experienced painful crises and needed to take medical leave. While she was away, her job was compromised and she had to reapply for a new position. Her old position had been phased out. It was in fact outsourced by another company. Katrina received no credit for her seniority status, was declined positions that she applied for and she subsequently received no other offers for employment. She then applied for unemployment. Katrina's husband was very supportive toward her in dealing with her condition and he obtained a second job to offset the loss in wages that were incurred due to her unemployment. Other problems occurred in their marriage and they reconciled their differences, however the stress was overwhelming for Katrina and she and her husband parted.

Katrina was aware of her illness and she tried to take care of herself. Her parents were always available whenever she needed them. As a young adult, she changed her diet and began to eat a lot of junk food. She was a social drinker when she socialized with her friends and her stress level increased. Katrina began to experience more frequent episodes of painful crises during this time. For 10 years, she was in and out of the hospital from the ages of 26 to 36. She went to Grady Hospital for tests to determine the cause of her constant illness. Their findings were that the emotional stress from her marriage contributed to her health issues. In addition to the pain medication that she took at home, she was prescribed ms contin, a low dose of morphine. This combined with morphine given during her hospitalization created a physical dependency. She took this medication for 8 years, however after a crises was over, she stopped taking the medication. She went through withdrawal and experienced vomiting and diarrhea. Katrina came to terms with her condition and she decided to find other means to control her painful crises and she stopped taking ms contin. With the help and support of her family, she was able to overcome her drug dependency.

She obtained a degree in accounting and was hired as a CPA and worked for a year. Another painful episode occurred and Katrina was hospitalized and put in ICU. She was given morphin for pain. She knew that she would die if she didn't make some changes in her life and she was determined to do just that. She began by making small changes like eating healthier and taking a multivitamin. She started to rest more and cut down on social drinking. Katrina stated that she got serious about her religious life. She realized that after her divorce, depression set in and she was ill more often. She lost several jobs due to time off because of her condition. She obtained disability through Social Security and Medicaid. Once Katrina made healthy adjustments to her lifestyle and identified her stress triggers, she experienced fewer episodes of crises. She reapplied to AFLAC and she was hired. She didn't have a major attack for 2 or 3 years. Ms. Murdix learned to manage her condition and she experienced successes along the way. However, while she was attending a social engagement in Las Vegas, she became ill and was hospitalized. Her mother flew to Las Vegas to take care of her. In remembering that attack, Katrina said that she had become overheated and she had 1 drink of alcohol. She over exerted herself and she was dehydrated. The stress of waiting for cabs and other inconveniences caused her to have a painful episode. She came back to Columbus and met a lady at Church who prayed for her. Katrina's will to make herself well and to depend on God brought about a new beginning for her. She began to tell others about her healing and how her faith in God and her prayer life brought it about. She wasn't sick for 1 or 2 years and then a crises landed her in the hospital again. While she was in the hospital, she shared with her roommate about her spiritual life and her faith in God.

Katrina stated that "things happen for a reason and that you can't relate to others unless you go through and experience some things for yourself"

Her health is stable, (last year was the last time that she was in the hospital).

April, this year she married her 2nd husband and she is maintaining her health and control of Sickle Cell Anemia.

-- <u>LEGACY</u> --

Samuel James was a fighter in so many ways. He fought the good fight of faith. He overcame obstacles in his life both physical and mental. He managed his condition as well as he knew how and he was congenial with others along the way. With his humble, quiet demeanor he won the hearts of many as he proclaimed the truth of the Gospel of Jesus Christ. He carried that spirit that he acquired early on in life, as he traversed from day to day and he braved his hardships like the astute man that he was. Rest now Samuel, we will see you again!!

Sickle Cell Anemia affects so many peoples' lives, not only the patient but their family members as well. Although in Africa it was thought to be a curse to the family, to be affected by sickle cell anemia, it is quite the contrary. All of life's experiences are a blessing from God. It doesn't matter whether our trials are great or small, God in His Word guides us through life every step of the way. "Footprints in the Sand" describes just How and Who does the carrying.

Yes, Samuel lived with Sickle Cell Disease and he left this life at a relatively young age, but he lived a good life and he was truly happy and well loved.

It matters not how long we live but the quality of our lives that counts.

Vera James

November 27, 2010

Ode to Samuel

"Hold to God's unchanging hand", is a spiritual song appropriate for this occasion. Its lyrics are: Time is filled with swift transition, naught of earth unmoved shall stand, build your hopes on things eternal, hold to God's unchanging hand.

Samuel held to God's unchanging hand when he saw a godly example in the home. This example was magnified, here, when he was baptized for the remission of sins. I remember Samuel preaching at the young men's service with the aid of a stool. It inspired me.

However, time is filled with swift transition. One day we are full of life's vitality and the next we are stricken without strength. Paul says, *"O wretched man that I am! Who shall deliver me from the body of this death? Rom. 7:24. 'The body of this death' is a frail and temporary life. This life was placed on us through the actions of Adam. Gen. 3:8.* The Bible calls life a vapor. James says, *"For what is your life? It is even a vapour, that appeareth for a little time, and then vanisheth away." James 4:14.*

This life is here today and gone tomorrow; yet full of pain. II Cor. 4:18. Enduring pain is not a pleasant experience. Psalm 32:3. Suffering with it depends on its intensity and degree. It may be slight, extreme or torturous. Job 33:19. Pain can be so severe that it can have a lasting effect on the mind.

Job in the 2nd chapter experienced this. His pain was so great that some even mourned for his death. Job's suffering was intense it affected his mind. His outlook began to waver. It is written in Job 3;1, *"After this opened Job his mouth, and cursed his day."* He sums up his own afflictions, saying: *"Man that is born of a woman is of few days, and full of trouble. He cometh forth like a flower, and is cut down: he fleeth also as a shadow, and continueth not." Job 14:1-2*

God had mercy on Job. Job 42:10.

Samuel had great battles with pain. His troubles not only affected him, but his family also. His health care issues were tremendous. His walk through life was full of pain. I can imagine how he must have identified with David as he cried unto the Lord saying, *"Have mercy upon me, O LORD; for I am weak: O LORD, heal me; for my bones are (vexed) in pain. Psalm 6:2.*

Though many judge, no one knows the inner struggle. Thus we sing, *'If by earthly friends forsaken---Still more closely to Him cling.'* God *is the discerner of the thoughts and intents of the heart. Heb. 4:12.* He had mercy on Job; he can have mercy on Samuel.

Therefore the inner spirit must hold on to God's spirit. Embracing the spirit of God is having faith in eternal things. Heb. 11:1' II Cor. 5:7. The sacred selection says, 'Build your hopes on things eternal---Hold to God's unchanging hand. God's unchanging hand is that same spirit that moved men to write the Bible. That same spirit that raised up Christ and that same spirit that will raise us up. *Rom. 8:11* says, *"But if the spirit of him that raised up Jesus from the dead dwell in you, he that raised up Christ from the dead shall also quicken your mortal bodies by his spirit that dwelleth in you."*

We acquire that spirit by seeking the Word of God. Our hymn says,

'Seek to gain the heavenly treasures—They will never pass away.' The Word of Jesus leads to heavenly treasure. He says, *"Heaven and earth shall pass away, but my words shall not pass away."* Matt. 24:35. Jesus is everlasting truth. He says, *"and, lo, I am with you always, even unto the end of the world. Matt. 28:20.* Every time we search the truth it inspires us. *"All scripture is given by inspiration of God, and is profitable for doctrine, for reproof, for correction, for instruction in righteousness: That the man of God may be perfect, thoroughly furnished unto all good works."* II Tim. 3:16. Every time we apply the truth it dwells in us. *"Let the word of Christ dwell in you richly in all wisdom; teaching and admonishing one another in psalms and hymns and spiritual songs, singing with grace in your hearts to the Lord."* Col. 3:16.

At this very minute we are teaching and admonishing through, song verses, 'When your journey is completed—If to God you have been true.'

Samuel's journey is completed, may he now have rest. Jesus says, *"Come unto me, all ye that labour and are heavy laden, and I will give you rest. Take my yoke upon you, and learn of me' for I am meek and lowly in heart: and ye shall find rest unto your souls. For my yoke is easy, and my burden is light."* Matt. 11:28-30.

An easy yoke and a light burden are the spirit, the soul and the body placed in the LORD'S Church. In the Church or out of the Church, death claims us all. The spirit returns to God who giveth. Ecc. 12:7. The soul is received in paradise or torment. Luke 1:23 and the body goes back to the earth. Job 34: 15. We all must meet this home going. Samuel has blessed us with his. Such a blessing deserves God's merciful judgment. He knows who fought a good fight, who finished his course and who kept the faith. II Tim. 4:7. Samuel now stands before Him, as everyone shall. Heb. 9:27.

God's mercy is described in the words of Jesus, which says: *"Let not your heart be troubled: ye believe in God, believe also in me. In my Father's house are many mansions: if it were not so, I would have told you. I go to prepare a place for you. And if I go and prepare a place for you, I will come again, and receive you unto myself: that where I am, there ye may be also."* John 14:1-4.

May 8, 2010.

Sermon delivered by Bro. Steven Short at Samuel's home going service.

<u>More Memories of Sam</u>

Vernita Fleming Coates with the children
in front of our home in San Jose, California.
Reuben II, Eric, Tiffany and Samuel

Samuel with his son, Samuel Jr., Jazmine
(Reuben Jr.'s daughter), Isaac and Samantha
(Samuel's son and daughter).

More Memories of Sam

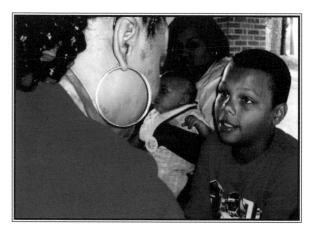

Tiffany talking to Samuel Jr.

Samuel Jr., Samuel, and father-Reuben Sr.

More Memories of Sam

Samuel with his daughter Samantha

More Memories of Sam

Alicia Hammonds with Samuel.

More Memories of Sam

More Memories of Sam

More Memories of Sam

Grandma, Tivvany, Grandpa,
Amari and Eric II.

For more information, further reading, internet addresses:

Sickle Cell Disease Association of America.
16 S. Calvert St. Suite 600, Baltimore, Md. 21202 (800) 421-8453.
iscdaa@sicklecelldisease.org; http://www.sicklecelldisease.org.

The Sickle Cell Information Center, P.O. Box 109, Grady Memorial Hospital, 80 Jessie Hill Jr. Dr. S.E. Atlanta, Ga. 30303;
(404) 616-3572. aplatt@emory.edu. http://www.scinfo.org/
Gillie, Oliver. Just the facts: Sickle Cell Disease.

Gold, Susan Dudley. Sickle Cell Disease

Harris, Jacqueline L. Sickle Cell Disease; *Murphy, Wendy.*
Orphan Diseases: New Hope for Rare Medical Conditions.

Platt, Allan F. and Alan Sacerdote. Hope and destiny: The Patients and Parent's Guide to Sickle Cell Disease and Sickle Cell Trait.

Watkins, Tionne. Thoughts. New York: Harper Entertainment 1999.

Bibliography

Silverstein, Alvin and Virginia, Silverstein, Laura Nunn.
The Sickle Cell Anemia Update.

Berkley Heights, N.J.: Enslow Publishers, Inc., 2006

Peterson, Judy Monroe. Sickle Cell Anemia. New York, N.Y. The
Rosen Publishing Group,

Sledge, Kaffie. Columbus Ledger and Enquirer. January 16, 1983,
p. E-1, E-2.

Bloom, Miriam, Ph. D. Understanding Sickle Cell Disease.

Jackson: University Press of Mississippi. 1995

Sickle Cell Anemia Encarta Online Encyclopedia. *Eckman, James*
R.B.A., M.D. 2001

<http://encarta:msm>

About the Author

Vera James attended Allegheny Community College in Pittsburgh, Pa. and Chattahoochee Valley Community College in Phenix City, Alabama. She is a former Operating Room Technician having worked in Pittsburgh, Pennsylvania; Napa, San Francisco and San Jose, California. She has been a Bible School teacher for over 30 years. Mrs. James has spoken at Ladies Day Programs at several congregations of the Church of Christ in Georgia. She was one of the youth leaders and the editor of the McCartha Drive Church of Christ bulletin for ten years. She is a Notary Public for the State of Georgia and she is presently employed as a Public Service Assistant at Mildred L. Terry Public Library in Columbus, Georgia.

This is Mrs. James' first book.

January 30, 1975 - May 4, 2010

CPSIA information can be obtained
at www.ICGtesting.com
Printed in the USA
252630LV00001B

9780578081625